Away in a MANGER

Front Cover: *Mary's Child* © Mark Missman. For print information, go to www.sagebrushfineart.com or call 801-466-5136.

Cover and interior designed by Christina Marcano
Cover design copyright © 2016 Covenant Communications, Inc.
Published by Covenant Communications, Inc.
American Fork, Utah

Printed in United States
First Printing: October 2016

25 24 23 22 21 20 19   10 9 8 7 6 5 4 3 2

ISBN: 978-1-52440-116-0

Away in a MANGER

Remembering His Sacred Birth
with Beloved Art and Music

AWAY IN A
manger,
no crib for
his bed,

THE
LITTLE
LORD

Jesus

laid down

his sweet head,

The stars
in the

heavens

LOOKED
DOWN

where he lay,

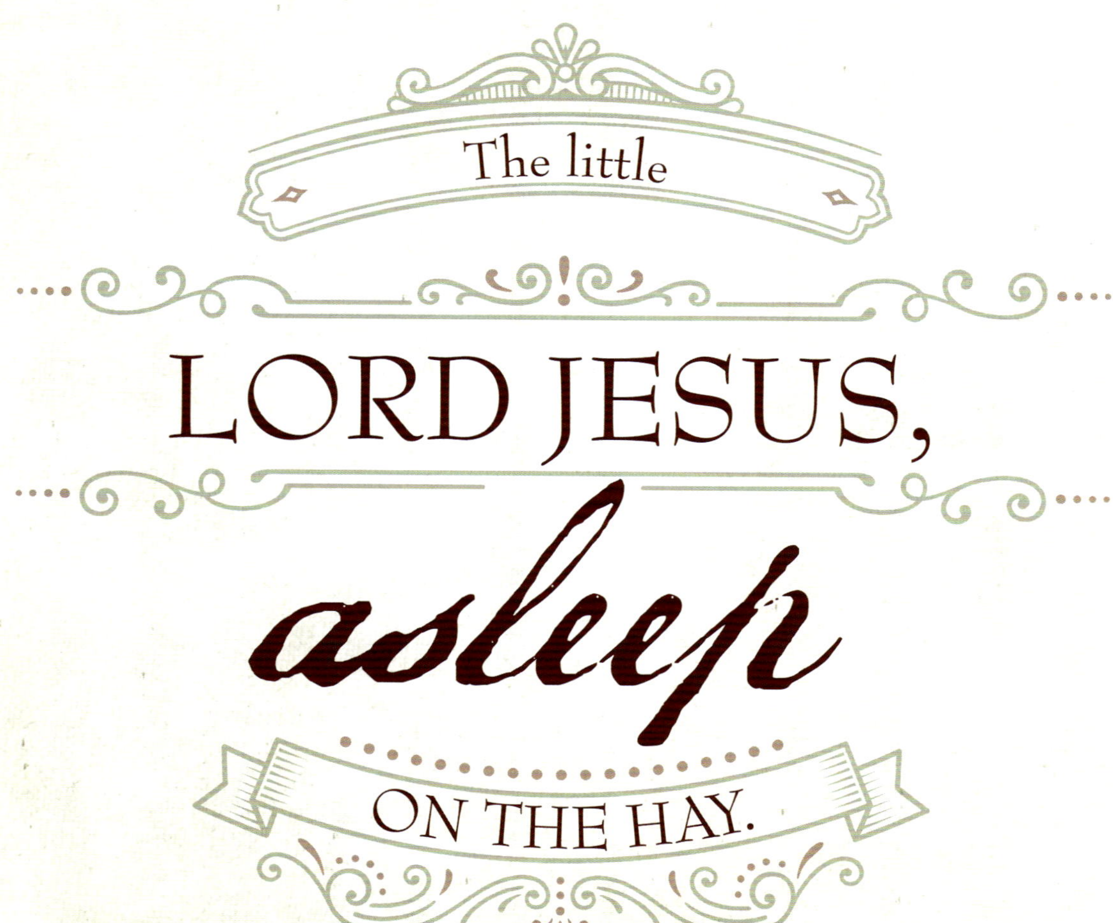

The little
LORD JESUS,
asleep
ON THE HAY.

The
cattle are lowing;
THE POOR BABY
WAKES,

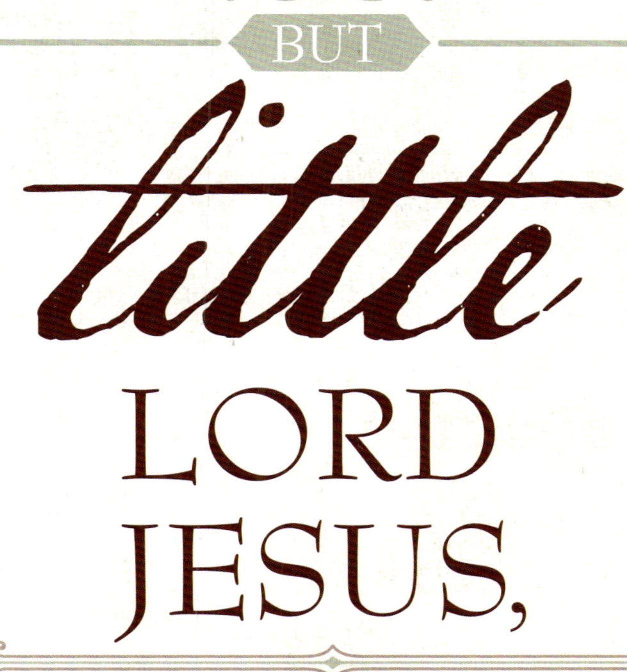

BUT
little
LORD
JESUS,
no crying he
MAKES.

I love thee,
LORD JESUS;
look down
from the sky

AND *stay* by my CRADLE till morning IS NIGH.

BE

near me,
LORD
JESUS;
I ask thee

TO STAY

CLOSE BY
ME
forever,
AND
love me,
I PRAY.

Simon Dewey

BLESS
ALL THE
dear
children
in thy
TENDER
CARE,

AND
FIT US
for
heaven,
to live
WITH
THEE
THERE.

ASLEEP,
asleep,
ASLEEP,
THE
Savior
in a stall!

ASLEEP,
asleep,
ASLEEP,
the
Lord of all.

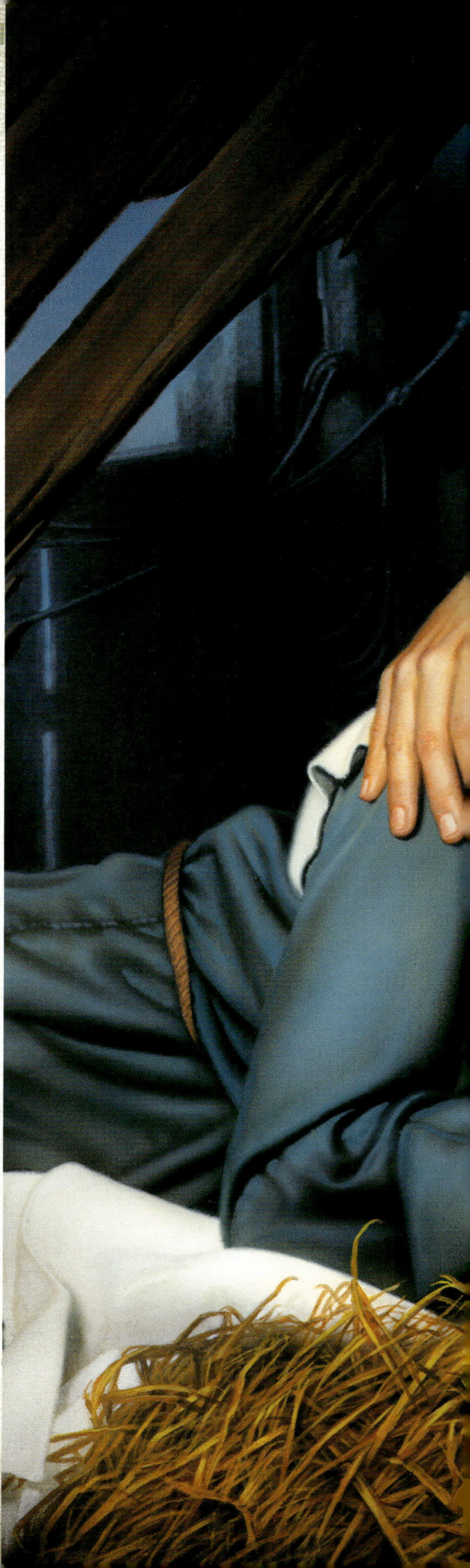

Away in a Manger

(Ver. 1)

Text: Anon., ca. 1883, Philadelphia
Music: William J. Kirkpatrick, 1838–1921;
harmonized by Rosalee Elser, b. 1925
Copyright © 1980 Rosalee Elser.

Used by permission. Making copies for one-time
noncommercial church or home use is permitted.

*QR code for music available on last page.

Luke 2:7
Luke 18:15–17

Away in a Manger

(Ver. 2)

*Chorus may be sung in one or two parts.

Luke 2:3–7
Luke 18:15–17

Words: attr. to Martin Luther, 1483–1546
Music: Charles H. Gabriel, 1856–1932

*QR code for music available on last page.

The Birth of the
CHRIST CHILD

Although we don't know all the details about what happened that night, this retelling—based on scriptural writing and the traditions of the day—is meant as a testimony of the reality of our Savior's birth.

Each year in Judaea, people were required by law to return to their hometown to be counted in a census and to pay their taxes. Just as Mary's baby was about to be born, she and her husband, Joseph, had to travel to Bethlehem to be taxed. It must have been a difficult and uncomfortable journey for Mary, who was so close to having her baby.

Mary's baby was no ordinary baby. Before she married Joseph, she was visited by an angel named Gabriel, who told her that Heavenly Father would be her baby's father. The angel also told her that she should name her baby Jesus. Both of these things had been taught by prophets for hundreds of years. The same angel visited Joseph, and he understood the things that were to happen even before he married Mary.

When Joseph and Mary arrived in Bethlehem, the town was already very crowded with people who had come to pay their taxes. Mary was so tired, and it was time for her baby to be born, but Joseph could not find a room at any of the inns in Bethlehem: they were already full. Joseph must have grown more and more worried about what would happen to them and where Mary's baby would be born. Finally one kind innkeeper could see what a hard thing Mary and Joseph were facing; he told Joseph that although all the rooms were full, he and Mary could stay in the stable where the animals were kept.

"And she brought forth her firstborn son, and wrapped him in swaddling clothes, and laid him in a manger; because there was no room for them in the inn."

—Luke 2:7

The stable was not likely what Mary and Joseph had hoped for. It was dirty, it probably smelled bad, and it was filled with animals such as cows and sheep. But at least it gave Mary some privacy and a sheltered place where she could give birth to her baby. Joseph must have done everything he could to make her comfortable, creating a soft bed from clean hay.

There were no doctors or nurses to help Mary on that sacred night; she and Joseph labored together to bring her holy baby—the Savior of all mankind—into the world. With all the love that every mother feels when she first meets her baby, Mary took Jesus into her arms and wrapped Him in swaddling clothes—strips of cloth that protected Him, kept Him warm, and helped Him feel secure. And so it was that Mary and Joseph and the animals in the stable that night were the first to see the tiny baby who would someday save us all.

"And the angel said unto them, Fear not: for, behold, I bring you good tidings of great joy, which shall be to all people. For unto you is born this day in the city of David a Saviour, which is Christ the Lord. And this shall be a sign unto you; Ye shall find the babe wrapped in swaddling clothes, lying in a manger."

—Luke 2:10–12

There was no crib in the stable. So Joseph and Mary made a bed for the baby in a manger—a trough used to hold feed for the animals in the stable. Never before or since has a manger been used for such an important purpose.

Jesus's birth was not the only miracle that night. A star brighter than any that had ever been seen in the nighttime sky bathed that little stable in Bethlehem with a light as brilliant as daylight, marking the place where Jesus had been born. It beckoned to the faithful, showing the way, inviting them to see for themselves that the day had come that the prophets had promised since the beginning of the world.

Humble shepherds tending their flocks on the hills around Bethlehem marveled at the star, then saw an angel surrounded by magnificent light. Not knowing what had just happened in that nearby stable, they were scared. But the angel told them not to be afraid: he shared the wonderful news that the Savior had been born and told the shepherds where to find the baby. The night skies filled with a choir of angels, and the shepherds hurried down the rocky hills to see for themselves the wonder long foretold.

On that same night, Wise Men from the East also saw the star. They too started their journey, bearing gifts for the Christ child.

Jesus, the baby born that night in the stable, became the Redeemer, the One who would make it possible for all of us to return and once again live with Heavenly Father. How meaningful that He was born in such a poor and lowly place—for His gift to us is for *all* of us, not just the rich or powerful or important. He came to save us all: every one.

That in itself is the wonder. He lives, even today, to comfort and heal and rescue all of us—a king who was born not in a palace or a mansion where only a few could be admitted, but in a quiet and humble stable, where each of us can share the joy of the miracle of all miracles.

Simon Dewey

Art Credits

P. iv: *Nativity* © Simon Dewey. Courtesy of Altus Fine Art. For print information, visit www.altusfineart.com.

P. 2–3: *Mary's Child* © Mark Missman. For print information, go to www.sagebrushfineart.com or call 801-466-5136.

P. 4–5: *Silent Night* © Joseph F. Brickey. For more information, go to www.josephbrickey.com.

P. 7: *For Unto Us a Child Is Born* © Simon Dewey. Courtesy of Altus Fine Art. For print information, visit www.altusfineart.com.

P. 8–9: *The Young Messiah* © Liz Lemon Swindle. Used with permission from Foundation Arts. For print information, go to www.foundationarts.com or call 1-800-366-2781.

P. 10–11: *In the Hands of the Father* © Roger Loveless. For more information, go to www.rogerlovelessart.com.

P. 12: *The Light of the World* © 2016 Jay Bryant Ward. For print information, go to www.jaybryantward.com.

P. 14–15: *Silent Night* © Liz Lemon Swindle. Used with permission from Foundation Arts. For print information, go to www.foundationarts.com or call 1-800-366-2781.

P. 16–17: *Dear to the Heart of the Shepherd* © Joseph F. Brickey. For more information, go to www.josephbrickey.com.

P. 19: *In the Arms of Mary* © Simon Dewey. Courtesy of Altus Fine Art. For print information, visit www.altusfineart.com.

P. 20–21: *A Savior Is Born* © Joseph F. Brickey. For more information, go to www.josephbrickey.com.

P. 22–23: *The Nativity* © David Lindsley. For more information, go to www.davidlindsley.com.

P. 25: *He Sent His Son* © Mark Missman. For print information, go to www.sagebrushfineart.com or call 801-466-5136.

P. 26–27: *His Name Shall Be Called Wonderful* © Simon Dewey. Courtesy of Altus Fine Art. For print information, visit www.altusfineart.com.

P. 29: *She Shall Bring Forth a Son* © Liz Lemon Swindle. Used with permission from Foundation Arts. For print information, go to www.foundationarts.com or call 1-800-366-2781.

P. 32: *They Call His Name Jesus* © Dan Freed. For more information, visit DanFreedWorks.com or call 801-916-2862.

P. 35: *In the Arms of Joseph* © Simon Dewey. Courtesy of Altus Fine Art. For print information, visit www.altusfineart.com.

Song Version 1, pg. 28

Song Version 2, pgs. 30–31